I0692464

Philip Francis

A State of the British Authority in Bengal

Under the Government of Mr. Hastings

Philip Francis

A State of the British Authority in Bengal
Under the Government of Mr. Hastings

ISBN/EAN: 9783337192426

Printed in Europe, USA, Canada, Australia, Japan

Cover: Foto ©ninafisch / pixelio.de

More available books at **www.hansebooks.com**

A

S T A T E

OF THE

BRITISH AUTHORITY IN BENGAL

UNDER THE GOVERNMENT OF

Mʀ. H A S T I N G S,

EXEMPLIFIED IN THE PRINCIPLES
AND CONDUCT OF

THE MARHATTA WAR,

AND HIS

N E G O C I A T I O N S

WITH

MOODAJEE BOOSLA,

RAJAH of BERAR.

From authentic Documents.

L O N D O N:

Printed by H. S. WOODFALL:
Sold by R. Baʟᴅᴡɪɴ, Paternoſter-Row.
M DCC LXXXI.

TO THE

COURT of DIRECTORS

OF THE

EAST INDIA COMPANY.

GENTLEMEN,

THE following papers, as far as they lay claim to YOUR attention, ſhould rather ſerve to remind, than to inform. I am perſuaded that your ineſtimable archives are conſulted by you, without remiſſion: and doubtleſs, the lights, which are there only to be obtained, alone decide your judgment and your conduct in all intereſts of the Company. It is to be lamented, that all acceſs to this great ſource of information ſhould be rigorouſly refuſed to the Public. The cauſe of truth and juſtice can rarely profit by concealment. It is the natural tendency, and, too often, the infamous

A 2 purpoſe,

purpofe, of that dark myfterious policy which fhuns examination, to perpetuate error, to render abufes inveterate, and to fhelter crimes.

Impreffed with thefe fentiments, I fhall make no apology for bringing forward to Public notice the character of the Government of Bengal, under the adminiftration of Mr. HASTINGS. I have not hefitated to fhew, in one ftriking inftance of internal arrangement *, that the contempt with which this Gentleman has uniformly received the commands of the Court of Directors, is fyftematical, and that He bids defiance to his mafters upon Principle. I fhall now venture to produce him on the fcene in his career of Conqueft; and fhall prove that, in Peace and War, he is *equally* your Servant; that he has the fame Maxims for the

* See a State of the Britifh Authority in Bengal.

Field

Field and for the Cabinet, and that He
is alike happy in bearing away the Palm
of civil and military Difobedience. To
compleat the Monument of this Gentleman's political fame, it will be a pleaf-
ing labour, to fhew that the fame gene-
rous difdain of his Superiors has accompanied him through all the Manœuvres
of *his* Syftem of finance; to difplay *his*
Skill in improving, *his* Tendernefs in fof-
tering, *his* Prudence in difpenfing, the
Treafure of the Provinces of whofe Wel-
fare he is appointed the Tutelary Guar-
dian.

I am aware that, to the common Reader, thefe fuggeftions may appear unfair,
and thefe Imputations cruel. But you,
Gentlemen, will not refufe to bear tefti-
mony to my Candour. The Court of
Directors have long been acquainted with
the true complexion of this Governor's
Principles. In the Company's General
letter

letter to Bengal, dated the, 23d of December 1778, his conduct in various inftances, is qualified by the Epithets, " INDECENT, PRESUMPTUOUS, UNWARRANTABLE, ILLEGAL," and in the letter from the Court of Directors to Bengal, dated the 14th of May 1779, the Expedition which makes the fubject of the following fheets, is treated as a direct Violation of PRUDENCE, POLICY, and GOOD FAITH.

If now it fhould be afked, by fome fimple Obferver of human Actions, upon what Principles we are to explain this ftrange, but continued, feries of reproach and confidence, of cenfure and reward, I muft own I fhould unwillingly attempt the folution of fo unnatural a phenomenon. The Abbé Raynal, fpeaking of the Decline of the Dutch Eaft India Company, and accounting for it, cites the following remarkable circumftance. " The
" contempt

" contempt of decency was puſhed ſo far,
" that a Governor General finding himſelf
" convicted of having pillaged the Trea-
" ſury to an enormous exceſs, was not
" afraid to juſtify his conduct, by pro-
" ducing a full Power ſigned by the Ma-
" nagers of the Company at home." You
have now a favourable opportunity of
removing far from yourſelves the ignomi-
ny of the application; and of conſoling the
Public, by the Reſolutions You are about
to take, with the hope that the preſent
Court of Directors will neither be inſen-
ſible to their Duty or careleſs of their Honor. It ſhall be my Province, Gentlemen,
to ſuggeſt freſh objects for the Exerciſe of
Your Political Wiſdom and Patriotic Virtue.

THE EDITOR.

ADVERTISEMENT.

IT is thought needlefs to make any Apology for the Form in which thefe Documents are given to the Public. Perfons converfant in India Affairs will even draw a Proof of their Authenticity from their prefent Arrangement.

*** A printed copy of thefe Documents was fent to each Member of the Court of Directors on Tuefday the 2d Inftant, a day appointed by them for enquiring into the fubject to which they relate. In the prefent edition a fmall alteration is made in the arrangement of the Extracts from Confultations, for the purpofe of rendering them more intelligible to the common reader. There is no change in the Matter or Facts.

Jan. 16, 1781.

A STATE

A

S T A T E

OF THE

BRITISH AUTHORITY IN BENGAL

UNDER THE GOVERNMENT OF

Mr. H A S T I N G S,

THE abſtracts annexed will ſerve for an in-
dex to the Conſultations, and to point out
ſuch parts of them as may deſerve particular attention, whenever it ſhall be thought fit to make
formal and regular inquiry into the whole tranſ-
action. The principles and conduct of the
meaſure are minutely canvaſſed in the minutes
of the minority. It may be uſeful, however,
to collect into one view ſome of the moſt ſtriking
circumſtances belonging to both.

I. The original reſolutions of the Governor
General and Council of the 2d of February,
1778, for ſupporting Bombay, profeſs to have
in view the reſtoration of Ragoba, conformable
to the plan communicated in a letter from that
Preſidency of the 12th of December, 1777, but
in no ſhape to violate the treaty of Poona. In
their ſubſequent letter of the 20th of January,
1778, they inform the Board that the overtures

B   made

made by the Ministerial Chiefs had produced no
effect, and that *they had immediately resolved that
nothing could be done* unless Sucuram Baboo joined in the application, which he never has done.
This Board, nevertheless, persist in sending the
detachment across India, but now take other
ground to justify the measure, viz. a supposed
connection between the French and the Poona
government.

II. The principal proof of this connection,
repeatedly urged and insisted on by Mr. Hastings, was, that the Marhattas had given the
port of Choul, near Bombay, to the French.
Yet, notwithstanding the peremptory assertions
so often used by the Governor on this subject,
and notwithstanding Monsieur Bellecombe, so
long ago as January last, was said to have gone
in person to take possession, the French, at
this hour, are not masters of Choul, nor ever
likely to possess it. In the same spirit, and for the
same purpose, the negociations of Monsieur St.
Lubin have been urged, and represented in the
most formidable point of view. At this distance
from England, a cloud of words is sufficient to
veil, diminish, or magnify any object, to suit
the wishes and designs of men in power here. In
the present instance, the Court of Directors
will find lights enough in the Consultations of
the Board, to shew them with what boldness and
facility facts are supposed, discoloured, and ex-
aggerated,

aggerated, and the moft alarming, as well as chimerical confequences deduced from them. They will judge whether Mr. Haftings, on his own ftate of facts, has taken meafures fuitable to the occafion ; whether the march of an army into the heart of Indoftan could, at any time, have had any other object but a union with Moodajee Boofla; and whether this object was not carefully kept out of fight, till either the de-tachment might be fo far advanced as not to be able to retreat with fafety, or till other circum-ftances fhould arife which might furnifh preten-ces for adopting a new fyftem, or rather for dif-covering the true purpofe of the perfons who planned the expedition. This obfervation kept in view, will ferve for a leading clue through all the windings of this extraordinary tranf-action.

III. In the courfe of the proceedings it will appear, that when the march of a reinforcement to Bombay was refolved on, Mr. Francis con-ftantly urged that it ought to be fent from Ma-dras by the way of Anjano, and replaced, if neceffary, from Bengal ; and that the Prefidency of Bombay recommended this mode, *as the beft and eafieft*. In feveral of Mr. Haftings's mi-nutes, particularly one of the 12th of October, the Court of Directors will fee how affectedly this propofition has been flighted, and what fort of arguments have been urged againft it. Mr. Haftings affirms, " that it did not even deferve

confideration ;

" consideration; and that, with superior dif-
" ficulties, and a dangerous navigation, the
" march from Pondicherry would exceed that
" from Culpee in length by one third of the
" distance." Yet the route by Anjango is well
known, and has been repeatedly used by detach-
ments to and from Bombay. The battalion of
Sepoys, which marched about February, 1774,
to join Colonel Keating, followed this route,
and arrived at Bombay without the loss of a
man; and even the Governor General himself,
on the 2d of February, 1778, proposed a letter
to the Presidency of Fort St. George, in which
the earnest desire of this Government is expressed,
that they should order the detachment, applied
for by the President and Council of Bombay, to
march immediately to their assistance.

With this evidence before the Court of Directors of the facility of the route by Anjango,
and considering that the strength of this detachment, added to the Madras army, might with
ease have swept all the French settlements on
both coasts, and saved the greatest part of the
blood and treasure which Pondicherry has cost,
they are to judge what motives but that which
I have assigned could possibly have determined
Mr. Hastings to send the detachment through
an immense unknown continent, in preference
to a route so perfectly known, and constantly
practised.

IV. The

IV. The feafon in which the troops were to march was as ftrenuoufly objected to by the minority as the route. In reply to this objection, the Court of Directors will fee with what perfeverance Mr. Haftings has maintained, that no feafon could be more happily chofen than the beginning of May: That the violent heats would foon be over, and that the fucceeding rains would be a relief to the troops, and facilitate the march. To thofe who have experienced the rains of India, this idea will undoubtedly appear new and extraordinary. Colonel Leflie's letters, particularly his private ones, will fhew that nothing in fact could be fo ill founded. He uniformly attributes the delay of his march to the torrents of rain which had overflowed the country, deftroyed the roads, and made even fmall rivers and nullas impaffable: light troops, without incumbrance, may perhaps move in any feafon; but it is not eafy to convey a train of artillery, with ftores, ammunition, campequipage, and provifions for a body of people not lefs than 36,000 in number, in a tempeftuous feafon, and through a country interfected with numberlefs ftreams, if not generally overflowed.

V. In the Confultation of the 12th of October, the Court of Directors will obferve what violent cenfures are thrown upon the Prefidency of Bombay, and how much pains are taken to

fix

fix upon *them* the responsibility of every miscarriage that has happened, or that may happen hereafter in the operations of the detachment. " They have done nothing ; they have attempt- " ed nothing ; they have neither availed them- " selves, nor wish to avail themselves of events ; " they have no instrument left, nor any inclina- " tion to seek for one. In short, we are aban- " doned by them, after all that we have done " for their relief."

The minority have no concern in the charges now exhibited against the Presidency of Bombay, nor does it belong to *them* to undertake their defence. Mr. Francis saw, and insisted on, the weakness and unsteadiness of their councils, at a point of time, (22d June, 1778) when more was in the power of the Board than barely to lament the effects of them. It rests with Mr. Hastings to account for, and justify, his conduct, in leaving the army, as he does, under the guidance of a Council, on whose prudence, steadiness, and activity, he at the same moment professes to place so little dependence.

VI. The Court of Directors will undoubtedly consider the enormous expence, as well as all the other consequences likely to attend this measure. The staff; the stores; a train of artillery, and allowances and supplies of all sorts, regulated solely by the commanding officer's direction, and the whole charge of the detachment

ment to be defrayed by remittances on this government. In the beginning of October, when Col. Goddard took the command, the military cheft was empty; fo that at that time they muft have fpent twelve lacks, which were to have carried them to Bombay, befides the advances of fubfiftence which the feveral battalions muft have received before they began their march. What the total expence of the meafure will amount to, or when it will end, can only be the fubject of very alarming conjectures. It is only in its infancy at prefent; yet if, in addition to the direct charge of moving with fuch a body of troops out of Bengal, a due proportion of the augmentation here is carried to the fame account as it ought to be, I prefume that thirty lacks * will not much exceed the real expence already incurred by the meafure. It is a growing expence; fince every ftep the detachment takes from our frontier removes it fo much the further from any poffible check or controul over its difburfements.

VII. The private correfpondence carried on between the Governor General and the commanding officer ought certainly to be an object of confideration. It is very difficult and diftref-

---

* On the 1ft of March, 1780, the detachment, together with the parties under Major Carnac and Captain Popham, had coft the Company upwards of 82 lacks, independent of remittances to Bombay.

fing

fing to thofe members of the Council, who dif-
approve of fuch a proceeding, to exprefs their
difapprobation of it in terms that do not imply
perfonal diftruft of their Prefident. There is no
language in which a total want of confidence in
his perfonal honor and veracity can be con-
veyed without a direct affront to him.

Mr. Francis, in his minute of the 16th of
November, has objected to the continuance of
this correfpondence, in the moft guarded and
moderate terms; but it was rather with a view
to exculpate himfelf, than with any hope of in-
fluencing Mr. Haftings's conduct. The prac-
tice is fo evidently wrong, and open to fo many
obvious ill confequences, that it requires no
illuftration. The Court of Directors are to
confider what fair and juftifiable purpofe it can
poffibly anfwer.

By Colonel Leflie's private letters, which Mr.
Haftings was, in fome fort, compelled to lay
before the Board on the 22d of October, (tho'
not accompanied with his own, as they ought
to have been) it appears, that he poffeffed information, in many inftances, which ought to
have been communicated directly and immediately to the Board. The letter of the 30th of
July in particular, eftablifhes two very material facts. 1ft, That whereas Mr. Francis appears, on the face of the Confultations to ob-
serve

ferve Colonel Leflie's conduct with attention, and to cenfure it with fome degree of feverity, while Mr. Haftings conftantly fupports and defends him; it is neverthelefs true, that at leaft as early as the end of June, Mr. Haftings muft have thought infinitely worfe of Col. Leflie's character and conduct than even Mr. Francis, who had no lights to guide him but the public letters.

2dly, That whereas Mr. Haftings about the end of June, if not fooner, muft have conceived the very worft opinion poffible of Col. Leflie, he takes no ftep to remove him from the command till the 12th of October, when, in all probability, he had heard of his death, or at leaft that there was no chance of his recovery: fo that, on his own principles, he muft have left the conduct of this moft important enterprize in the hands of a man whom he does not fcruple to accufe in the groffeft manner of *ignorance, prefumption, and rapacity.* In return however, the Court of Directors will obferve, that Colonel Leflie expreffed no apprehenfion of the Governor's refentment, or of any effects it can produce; but on the contrary, fets him at defiance in plain terms, and refufes to correfpond with him any longer.

VIII. Suppofing it poffible that every objection to the meafure, on the fcore of prudence or expediency, could be anfwered, or removed;

C or

or that any degree of fuccefs fhould hereafter furnifh an unexpected argument in its defence, there is ftill another, and a moft important point of view, in which it becomes the Company's dignity and wifdom to confider it.

When Mr. Haftings engages the Company's arms in offenfive wars without neceffity; when he complicates their government in treaties and alliances with the Indian powers, of which war, acquifition, and conqueft are the fole ob- ject; when he fends their troops far away from the defence of their territories; when he difturbs the peace of India; and when he avows his vain ambitious purpofes fo far as to declare that, " * If the Britifh arms and influence have fuf- " fered a fevere check in the Weftern world, " it is the more incumbent on thofe who are " charged with the interefts of Great-Britain " in the Eaft, to exert themfelves for the re- " trieval of the national lofs; that we have " the means in our power; and that with fuch " fuperior advantages as we poffefs over every " power which can oppofe us, *we fhould not* " *act merely on the defenfive*;" does he not fubvert the fundamental principles of the Com- pany's policy; does he not difobey their re- peated and moft peremptory orders, and tranf- grefs every line of limitation, which they had prefcribed to their fervants for the adminiftra-

* Confultation, 22d June, 1778.

tion

tion of their affairs ? If the affirmative ſhould appear true, the Court of Directors will un-doubtedly recall to their remembrance the prin-ciples on which the Rohilla war was unani-mouſly condemned by them, and how groſsly their condemnation of that meaſure has been ſlighted. They will reflect on the nature and extent of the truſt repoſed in them by the Company, and by the nation ; and ſeriouſly conſider on how precarious a foundation the Britiſh empire in India ſtands ; when one daring individual can, at his pleaſure, ſubvert every principle of their government, violate their moſt poſitive orders and ſolemn inſtructions, contemn their authority, and ſet their power at defiance. It will not, I truſt, be too late for them to weigh the diſgraceful and dangerous conſequences of uniting conſtant condemnation with conſtant impunity in the perſons of Mr. Haſtings and Mr. Barwell, and of continuing two men in ſtations of the higheſt truſt and dignity, whom, if we may rely on the opinion they have repeatedly expreſſed of their conduct and character, they ought not to think worthy of the loweſt.

The motion of the 23d of November ap-peared ſome days after the preceding obſer-vations were drawn up. In addition to the re-marks made upon it in Mr. Francis's minute of the ſame day, the Court of Directors have only to compare it with the language held by

Mr.

Mr. Haftings on the 12th of October, and the indignation with which he pretended to refent a fufpicion expreffed by Mr. Francis, that the detachment was really never meant to proce d to Bombay.

"If there are men in England fo devoid of
"common fenfe, as to fuppofe it poffible for
"me to have formed a plan oftenfibly profeffed
"for the affiftance of Bombay, but really
"meant as a cover for other defigns, let them ;
"whoever they be, or in whatever relation they
"may ftand to this government, fuch opinions
"will give me no kind of concern."

In the latter part of this declaration, there is certainly no reafon to queftion his fincerity. The myftery is now unfolded, and all farther concealment either ufelefs or impracticable. The great original difficulty with Mr. Haftings was, to find pretences for fo extraordinary and queftionable a ftep, as that of fending an army out of thefe provinces into the heart of India. To remove it, no affertions were fpared, no artifice omitted, no fophiftry unemployed : That point once carried, and the decifive act of crof-fing the Jumna once done, the fcene changes.— New facts are afferted, new principles eftablifhed, and new objects propofed. The fame army which originally was to have reinftated Ragoba, and which, even fo late as the 15th of October, was ftill profeffedly deftined to fupport that
interest,

intereft, is now to place Moodajee Boofla at the head of the Marhatta Empire, and to join with him in an invafion of the Decan. At the fame time the neceffity of providing for the immediate fafety of Bombay againft a French invafion, which on the 12th of October was urged, and infifted on as a reafon for leaving the detachment under the command of that Prefidency, is totally forgotten. Yet there is no new fact of any kind before the Board to warrant a fuppofition that this object is lefs neceffary to be provided for at the prefent moment than it was on the 12th of October, when Mr. Haftings declared; " That if it was ne-" ceffary to ftrengthen the Prefidency of Bom-" bay when the firft idea of it was fuggeft-" ed, it was much more fo now, when we have " been told by the higheft Authority, that " a powerful armament has been prepared in " France, the firft object of which was an at-" tack upon Bombay ; and when we know " with moral certainty, that all the powers of " the adjacent continent are read to join the " invafion."

This ftate of facts, whether real or fuppofed, remaining unaltered, the powers given to the Prefidency of Bombay to call the detachment to their affiftance are revoked, and the army ordered to proceed to Berar, and to halt there. Yet now we find, by the laft letter from Poona, that

that the Prefident and Council of Bombay, rely-
ing on the repeated promifes of affiftance given
them by this government, had taken their final
refolution to act immediately againft the Marhattas; that is, in fupport of Ragoba's pretenfions to the fovereign power of the Marhatta ftate. At the fame time, fuppofing Colonel Goddard to have been able to penetrate
into Berar, and to have carried his inftructions
into execution, the faith of the company will
have been engaged to Moodajee Boofla, to fupport his pretenfions to the fame object; fo that
if no external impediment were to defeat the
operation of the oppofite principles on which
the two Prefidencies are now acting, it might
happen that one Englifh army might meet another in the field, and that the competitors
would have a right to infift upon the public
faith, feverally pledged to them, by the Company's reprefentatives, and to bring their refpec-
tive auxiliaries into action. To avoid this extre-
mity there can be no refource but treachery and
and breach of faith to one of the parties at leaft,
if not to both.

ABSTRACTS

A B S T R A C T S

F R O M

C O N S U L T A T I O N S.

Jan. 29, 1778. THE march of the detachment under the command
of Colonel Leſlie originated from a letter from
the Preſidency of Bombay, dated 12th of December, 1777, in which they give notice to the
Governor General and Council of an offer. in-
directly made them, by ſome members of the
Miniſterial Party, to reinſtate Ragoba, and of
their own determination to accept ſuch offer,
whenever it ſhould be authenticated by a direct
engagement from the Miniſters, and to march
with Ragoba to Poona.

On this day Mr. Francis entered a formal
proteſt againſt the proceedings of the Bombay
Preſidency. Mr. Haſtings propoſed a ſeries of
queſtions on the ſame ſubject, meaning that the
reſolutions thereupon ſhould be the baſis of the
future meaſures of the Board. The general
tendency of the queſtions was to approve their
conduct, and to promiſe them ſupport.

2d

2d February.—Mr. Haftings's queftions are confidered, and carried by his cafting voice. He then propofed to take General Stibbert's opinion on the means of fending a reinforcement to Bombay, and the propriety of augmenting the Sepoy corps ; and concluded with a preffing letter to Fort St. George, to induce them to forward a reinforcement from thence immediately to Bombay.

9th February.—Mr. Haftings informs the Board, that he has private intelligence that Monfieur Bellecombe is gone to the Malabar Coaft, with a view to take poffeffion of Choul, a port-town near Bombay, fuppofed to be ceded to the French by the Marhattas.

23d.—Read the Bombay letter of the 2cth of January, on which the Governor's motion for fending them a reinforcement by the way of Calpee appears to be founded. Mr. Francis and Mr. Wheeler protefted in the ftrongeft terms againft the refolution of the majority, which followed the motion.

13th March.—On the receipt of the Company's orders of the 4th of July 1777, Mr. Wheler and Mr. Francis joined in an addrefs to the Governor, and urged the Board to countermand the detachment, but without effect.

18th.

18th.—The majority fent orders and inftructions to the Prefidency of Bombay of the moft violent and hoftile tendency to the Poona government*, and equivalent in effect to a declaration of war with the Marhattas. Mr. Francis and Mr. Whèler entered their protefts, with their reafons.

30th.†—A regiment of cavalry, commanded by Lieutenant Colonel Goddard, ordered to join Leflie's detachment.

6th April. — The detachment ordered to march, though letters from Bombay reprefent every thing there in a ftate of tranquillity. No motion whatever yet made in favour of Ragoba, nor any effect or confequence from the pretended overtures on the part of the Minifters, mentioned in their letter of the 12th December, 1777.

11th May.—A letter from Bombay of the 5th of April, having advifed the Board of a revolution at Poona, by which Ragoba is faid to be re-eftablifhed, Mr. Francis moved, that the march of the detachment fhould be fufpended, as no longer neceffary. The majority perfift.

* Vide Confultations 23d March.
† Military Confultations 27th March.

D   16th,

16th. *—Mr. Francis again preffed the recall of the detachment, and continued the debate, but to no purpofe. (19th.) Mr. Haftings conftantly affirms that the rainy feafon is favourable to the march of the troops.

8th June.—Mr. Francis again urged the recall of the detachment, on account of the oppofition given to Leflie on croffing the Jumna, and the future difficulties he would probably meet with. Mr. Haftings in reply declared his *unalterable determination to profecute the meafure to the utmoft of his power to its conclufion.*

11th June.—Letter from Bombay, dated 2d May, to inform the Board, that they have fent an order to Leflie not to advance any further until he may again hear from them. This ftep is faid to be founded " on the opinion they have formed " on the prefent ftate of affairs, and their defire " to fave the Company from the heavy ex- " pence, and their troops from the dangers and " difficulties of a march from our provinces to " that fide of India."

21ft.—Letter from Bombay of the 9th of May, to inform the Board that they had reverfed the preceding refolution within two days after it was taken, and ordered the detachment

* Vide Confultations 21ft May.

to

to proceed; but no reafon is affigned for this alteration.

22d.—Confidering this extraordinary fluctuation in the councils of that Prefidency, and that no motives whatfoever were affigned for it, Mr. Francis reprefented to the Board the hazard and difcredit of leaving the detachment at the difcretion of fuch councils, and on that ground again urged the neceffity of recalling it; but in vain.

29th June.—Received a letter, dated 20th May, from Bombay, defiring, that for the future, any reinforcement to be fent them might proceed *directly from Madras, as the beft and eafieft mode.* It will appear hereafter, that about this time Mr. Haftings had intirely altered the extraordinary opinion he had hitherto poffeffed of Colonel Leflie's merit and qualifications.

6th July.—On this day Mr. Haftings made his firft direct move towards the object, which he fince appears to have had originally at heart, of an alliance with Moodajee Boofla, and which I think will appear to have been the real object of this expedition. Colonel Leflie is now ordered to take his route through Berar, inftead of the ftrait road through Malva, the Chief of which, Modajee Sindy, is now, for the firft time, known " to have had no connection with this

D 2 " government,

" government, and to have always been repre-
" fented as a partizan of Nana Furnefe."

7th.—Advices received this day from Cairo
of a war in Europe. The majority determine
that the detachment fhall halt in Berar.

9th July. — When the Board expected from
the Governor General a plan for the defence of
Bengal againft a French invafion, he produced,
inftead of it, a laboured hiftory of the Ram
Raja, the Conftitution of the Marhatta Empire, and Moodajee Boofla's rights or pretenfions to the fovereignty ; and concluded with
recommending that a Treaty of Alliance fhould
be formed with Moodajee Boofla, and that a
Company's Servant fhould be immediately deputed to him with full powers for that purpofe.

10th.—Mr. Wheler and Mr. Francis warmly
oppofed the meafure, and urged the neceffity of
putting Bengal in a ftate of defence, recalling
the detachment, and fending a reinforcement
from Madras to Bombay, to act folely on a defenfive plan.

11th.—Treaty of Alliance refolved on by the
majority, but the plan of it not produced—Mr.
Elliott appointed to conduct it,

18th.

18th.—Mr. Elliott's inftructions produced this day, and voted, notwithftanding the ftrongeft oppofition that could be given to the meafure by Mr. Francis and Mr. Wheler. It appears that Ragoba was to be laid afide, and Moodajee Boofla placed at the head of the Marhatta Empire, and fupported in his pretenfions againft the Subah of the Decan. This fcheme of operations is recommended by the Governor General, at the opening of a French war. During all this time the detachment halted at Chatterpour, a few days march from the Jumna. It appears by Colonel Leflie's private letters, that Mr. Haftings muft have been perfectly acquainted with his tranfactions, yet at the Board he conftantly defends him, and even recommends approving the attack of Mow, though *he* could not be unacquainted with the true motives of that barbarous meafure.

17th Auguft.—Received a letter from Bombay, dated 25th July, faying that they had declared the Treaty of Poona violated, and no longer binding on the part of the Company. That they had determined to accept the offers of Moraba, and other Chiefs who had declared in favour of Ragoba, and to march with him to Poona in the beginning of September. Mr. Haftings, notwithftanding his projected Treaty with Moodajee Boofla, approves their plan for reinftating Ragoba, yet reprefents his caufe as defperate,

defperate, and the conduct of the Prefidency of Bombay as *equivalent to a refolution to do nothing:* that is, he fupports their meafures, though againft his belief of their taking effect. By letters from Colonel Leflie, it appears that the Prefidency of Bombay have directed him to alter his route ; that is, not to proceed through Guzerat to Broach, or Surat, but to proceed more foutherly towards Poona.

31ft Auguft.—Some reflections having been made by Mr. Francis on Colonel Leflie's extraordinary delay at Chatterpour, the Board agreed with him, that the caufes of it deferved to be inquired into.

2d September.—In the courfe of a warm debate on Colonel Leflie's continuance at Chatterpour, Mr. Haftings uniformly defends and fupports him, and with much apparent confidence in Colonel Leflie's conduct, refers to the event to juftify it.

5th October.—From the 2d of September to this day, the Board had no material advices from Colonel Leflie. He had altered the pofition of his camp, but it did not appear that he had any ferious intention to continue his march. Mr. Francis urged that his conduct fhould be inquired into, but Mr. Haftings requefted that the inquiry might be deferred. On receipt of the

the news of Mr. Elliot's death, Mr. Haftings moved that the commiffion fhould be continued, and another perfon appointed to carry it into execution.

7th October.—This laft motion withdrawn by the Governor, who perfifts in his project of an alliance with Moodajee Boofla, but now declares *that it is always more advantageous to wait for folicitations than to make advances.* The new inftructions now propofed for the march of the detachment will be found to deferve the particular attention of the Court of Directors. In this place it is fufficient to remark, that they leave the army under the orders of the Prefidency of Bombay for two exprefs purpofes, viz. to fupport any plan or defign for the reftoration of Ragoba, or to provide for the immediate fafety of Bombay againft a French invafion. At this debate the majority, for the firft time, difcovered a diftruft of Colonel Leflie, with fome indirect profeffions of an intention to remove him.

12th Oct.—But, till this day, no refolution was taken to remove him from the command. The Governor now informs the Board, that it *had been the will of God to blaft his defigns by means which no human prudence could have forefeen, and againft which therefore he had provided no refource.* Yet he affirms, " that the effects of the
" detachment

" detachment will still answer his most sanguine
" hopes, and that the measure itself is as ad-
" visable now, and more so, than when it was
" first adopted."

19th Oct.—The last letter written by Colonel
Leslie, who died on the 3d of October, states
fully the causes which have retarded his march,
and accounts for his not having been hitherto
more explicit in his communication to the Board,
by saying, that " he had afforded Mr. Hastings,
" *at his own desire*, a particular journal of oc-
" currences, and trusted to him for such expla-
" nation as the Board might desire to know."

22d.—Mr. Hastings lays Colonel Leslie's private letters before the Board; that dated the 30th
of July deserves the most particular attention.

26th.—A letter from Bombay of the 11th of
September says, " that they have not taken any
" measures in prosecution of the plan communi-
" cated in their letter of the 25th of July, but
" that they shall now very speedily come to
" some decisive resolutions, and advise the Board
" immediately of the result."

2d November. *—Colonel Goddard proceeds
on his march to Sagur; finds the military chest

* Consultations 2d November.

empty,

empty, and draws bills on the treasury for the subsistence of the detachment.

12th.—The Governor proposes an arrangement for supplying the detachment with money, by remittances to Naugpore, the capital of Berar. If it be not intended that the army should halt in that country, the measure is absurd; for supposing their march to Bombay to be continued without interruption, they ought to arrive there before a remittance, now made from hence, can reach them. But the proposition supposes them to want money, and to receive it more than two months hence at least, at a place a thousand miles distant from the professed place of their destination.

16th.— A private letter from Colonel Goddard of the 22d of October, to Mr. Hastings, with others from Moodajee Boosla, and his Ministers, laid before the Board. The Governor proposes to renew the negotiation with Moodajee Boosla, on the principles of Mr. Elliott's instructions, and to commit the conduct of it to Colonel Goddard, with full powers to conclude. Mr. Francis and Mr. Wheler object to the private correspondence carried on between the Governor and the commanding officer of the Company's troops, and assign their reasons at large for dissenting from the motion. The resolution carried of course.

E 23d

23d November *. — A motion sent in circula-
tion by the Governor, to revoke the powers delegated on the 15th of October to the Presidency
of Bombay, of commanding the march of the
detachment. Mr. Francis and Mr. Wheler pro-
test against the motion, as not only inconsistent
with all the principles hitherto avowed, and
with the ostensible objects hitherto proposed to
be accomplished by the expedition, but as not
corresponding with, or capable of being justified
by the reasons assigned for it.

30th.—A letter from Mr. Lewis at Poona,
dated 27th October, containing the following
information : " By orders from Governor Horn-
" by, I have sent away all the Sepoys who came
" with Mr. Mostyn, and am in hourly expecta-
" tion of being recalled myself, as the Governor
" writes me that the Select Committee have de-
" termined on acting against this Government."

21st December, 1778.—From the 15th of
November to this day, the Board received but
one letter from Colonel Goddard, dated the 5th
of November; by which it only appears, that
he was engaged in hostilities with Balajee Pundit,
who harassed his march with five thousand Marhatta horse.

On the 21st of December Mr. Hastings
laid before the Board a private letter of the

* Vide Consultations 7th Dec.

16th

16th of November, from Colonel Goddard to himfelf; he was then at Burfea, 25 Cofs from the Narbudda; his march ftill interrupted, and his fupplies cut off by Balajee Pundit. He had received friendly letters from Moodajee Boofla, but obferves, "That it was plain he " would rather fome agreement had been en- " tered into before the arrival of the army in " his territory."

On the fame day Mr. Haftings produced a copy of a letter from Moodajee Boofla to Co-lonel Goddard, dated the 23d of November, which had been forwarded by Mr. Anderfon, directly from Nagpour to Calcutta. The contents of this letter are of the utmoft im-portance : He lays before Colonel Goddard, in the ftrongeft colours, a detail of the prepara-tions making by the Poona government to op-pofe his march, and of the dangers and diffi-culties which he muft expect to meet with. He declines joining him with a body of his troops, obferving, " That it could produce " no good effect, but would remove the veil " from the bufinefs, and leave their defigns " expofed; that it would deftroy the friend- " fhip *eftablifhed between him and the Peifhwa*, " *and Nizam ul Dowla*, and expofe his domi- " nions to the ravages of the armies of the " Decan in Berar and at the Gauts." Fi-nally, he advifes Colonel Goddard to write all thefe particulars to Calcutta, and wait for or-

ders

ders from thence; and, till their arrival, continue on the banks of the Nerbudda. In the
mean time he recommends it to him, to write
an amicable letter to the Peifhwa, to defire a
fafe paffage through his dominions to Bombay,
with affurances that the march of the detachment had no other object than to ftrengthen
that place againft the defigns of the French.

Mr. Haftings, after producing this letter, informed the Board that Moodajee Boofla had
been at the point of death, and added in dif-
courfe, that he was not the real Raja of Berar,
but only deputy to his fon.

Mr. Francis, finding that all this important
intelligence was not followed by any motion
from the Governor, propofed two queftions to
the Board; Firft; " That it appeared that
" Moodajee Boofla was not inclined to join
" Colonel Goddard; Secondly; " That it
" was his, Moodajee Boofla's, opinion, that the
" continuance of his march would be attended
" with the greateft difficulties and dangers."—
The object of thefe queftions, if they had not
been refolved in the negative, was to eftablifh
the affirmative, as a ground for recalling the
detachment, or fending it along the Nerbudda
to Broach.

By Moodajee Boofla's letter it appears, that
on the 23d of November, he had no idea of
breaking

breaking with the Poona Government; that he was alarmed for the fafety of his own country, and very unwilling to join Colonel Goddard, or to fuffer him to come into it. He fpeaks the language of a man of fenfe; but his letter difcovers no appearance * of *that approved bravery and fpirit* on which Mr. Haftings profeffes to reft his hopes, † *that he will ardently catch at the objects prefented to his ambition.* And though it be ftrictly true, as Mr. Haftings himfelf fays in his letter of the 23d November to the Raja's prime minifter, " *That in the whole of his conduct* " *he, Mr. Haftings, has departed from the com-* " *mon line of policy, and has made advances where* " *others in his fituation would have waited for fo-* " *licitation,*" it does not appear that all his advances have produced any favourable impreffion on the mind of Moodajee Boofla; at leaft they have hitherto had no material influence upon his conduct.

If, after all, this man be not the real Raja of Berar, it remains to be confidered whether the ftate of Berar can be bound by any act of his, or whether the alliance, offenfive and defenfive, which Colonel Goddard is directed to form with him in the terms of Elliott's inftructions, can be concluded with fafety or honour to this government, when it is allowed that one of the

* Vide his letter to Dewagur Punditt, 23d Nov. 1778.
† Ditto.

contracting

contracting parties has no right, in his own person, to conclude such an alliance.

28th Dec. 1778.—The Governor moves, that
two battalions may be ordered immediately from
the barracks near Calcutta, under the command
of Major Camac, to reinforce Colonel Goddard,
in order to supply all losses which the detachment may have suffered by Colonel Leslie's de-
lays, and by the length of their march. They
are to proceed to the western frontier of Pala-
mow, and there wait the directions of Goddard,
either for a junction with him for the protection
of Nagpour, or to preserve the communication
with these provinces.

Before the question was put, Mr. Francis de-
sired to see the returns of the detachment, that
the Board might know what loss it had really
suffered, and on what grounds the reinforcement
was proposed. No returns, no letters, nor
explanation of any kind, were produced. Mr.
Barwell expressly declared, " That there was no
" indispensible necessity to influence the propo-
" sition ; and that, if he was to form his opinion
" simply on the necessity of the thing, he
" should certainly vote against the march of the
" troops." Mr. Hastings, under colour of an
objection urged by Mr. Francis to the private
correspondence carried on between him and the
commanding officer, said, that he had been
thereby *discouraged from affording the Board, in*
their

their collective capacity, those lights which, upon many points, were neceſſary for their information. He then rambled into ſtrictures upon a ſuppoſed inconſiſtency in Mr. Francis's conduct, in laying an extract of a private letter before the Board in June laſt, yet objecting to the authority of private letters from the commanding officer to the firſt and executive member of the Go-vernment, and proteſting againſt their private correſpondence. The Minutes will ſhew, in what manner theſe reflections were anſwered.—In this place however, it may be proper to ob-ſerve, that Mr. Haſtings, notwithſtanding all his public declarations to the contrary, muſt have given credit to the extract above-men-tioned; ſince Colonel Leſlie, in his private letter of the 30th July, reproaches him with the more *than negative belief*, expreſſed in one of his own letters, *of the poſſibility of ſome accidental error having happened on the firſt day's march from Calpee,* and anſwered a queſtion put to him by the Go-vernor's order, which would have been an abſur-dity in terms, if Mr. Haſtings did not believe the fact, viz. *why the firſt day's march was ſo fatal?*

Other obſervations, of much greater conſe-quence, occur upon the proceedings of this day. A reinforcement is ordered, upon a ſim-ple preſumption, that the detachment has ſuf-fered a conſiderable loſs. No return or letters
are

are produced to prove it, and all lights avow-
edly withheld from the Board. Mr. Barwell,
at the same time, denies the neceſſity of the
meaſure; and Mr. Haſtings himſelf, in the
courſe of the debate, affirms, " that the loſs of
" men bears no degree of proportion to the
" reinforcement, and has in effect been incon-
" ſiderable." The purpoſe of this reinforcement muſt therefore be, to provide for the protection of Nagpour, or, as Mr. Barwell ex-
preſſes it, *to give that ſecurity to the dominions of
the Berar Chief as to diſpel every apprehenſion he
may entertain of the hoſtilities with which he may
be threatened.* From theſe explanations it is to
be underſtood, that the Raja of Berar, who,
with the aſſiſtance of the detachment, was to
overſet the Marhatta ſtate, and to invade the
Deccan, wants two battalions of our Sepoys for
the protection of his own capital, and the ſecurity of his dominions. There is, however, no
reaſon yet to believe, that this Raja is at all diſ-
poſed to avail himſelf of our aſſiſtance. On
this day the Board does not know whether Col,
Goddard has croſſed the Nerbudda or not.

30th Dec. 17⁻8.—The Governor moves, that
ſeven hundred draughts may be ſent with Major Camac to recruit Colonel Goddard's army,
and that they ſhould march *without arms or ammunition.* However, he was afterwards obliged
to yield to the remonſtrances of Mr. Wheler
and

and Mr. Francis on this point, and let the recruits march with their arms, and to move that
Camac might have two field pieces.

4th January, 1779.—The Governor informs
the Board, from a private letter of Colonel
Goddard, dated 30th of November, that he
was arrived at the banks of the Nerbudda, after
a fatiguing march, through difficult paſſes in the
mountains, and that he then ſaw no impediment
to his croſſing that river.

7th January.—A letter arrived from Colonel
Goddard of the 2d and 5th of December, informs the Board that he had croſſed the Nebud-
da, and was encamped on the ſouthern banks
of that river, within the territory of Berar,
where he waited to be informed of the Rajah's
final reſolutions. He ſays, that all the artillery
and gun-carriages were much ſhattered, and in
want of repair; but that the number of ſick was
reduced from a thouſand to about four hundred.
Letters received from Moodajee Booſla, and
his miniſters, of the 5th of December. Inſtead
of joining Colonel Goddard, the Rajah gives
Mr. Haſtings a great deal of good advice, both
moral and political, concerning the preſervation
of peace, fidelity to engagements, juſtice, cle-
mency, &c. but in particular, he recommends
it to him to act with deliberation, and to proportion his means to his end; obſerving, " that

F   " it

" it is a proverb, that whatever is deliberately
" done is well done."

On the whole it appears clearly by thefe letters, that the Rajah never had an idea of the nature or extent of Mr. Haftings's views, much lefs
of breaking with the Pefhwa and the Nizam, or
of entering into any engagements with this Government that could lead him to a rupture with
either of them. He vindicates the Pefhwa from
the defigns imputed to him by the Board, of a
fecret connection with the French, and offers his
mediation. This may be confidered as a ftep
towards taking a direct part with his country-
men, if his mediation be not acquiefced in. At
all events he difclaimed every thought of acting againft them. After enumerating the Chiefs
and their forces, who were prepared to oppofe
Colonel Goddard, he exprefsly fays, " The
" junction of a body of my forces with his
" would avail nothing in the face of fuch large ar-
" mies, but would only involve me in the greateft
" loffes; yet neither was it advifeable for him to
" return, which would diminifh the awe and
" refpect in which he was held." In the end
he fays, that " the times require that a concili-
" ation take place with the Poona minifters."

11th January.—Mr. Francis, finding that the
Governor General obferved a profound filence
on the fubject of Moodajee Boofla's letters, and
that no inftructions whatfoever were to be fent

to

to Colonel Goddard, after waiting till the council held this day was on the point of breaking
up, thought it neceffary to record a Minute, in
which his fentiments are ftated at large refpect-
ing Modajee Boofla's conduct, and the critical
pofition of the detachment. In this Minute the
contents of the above letters are ftrictly can-
vaffed, and a conclufion drawn from them, that
recailing the detachment would be the moft advifeable ftep to be taken in a fituation which
admits of no one eligible refolution. To this Minute the Governor declared he did not think it
neceffary or proper to reply. In a day or two
after the Board received the firft intelligence, by
way of Madras, of the motion of a detachment
from Bombay towards Poona, for the profeffed
purpofe of reinftating *Ragoba*.

January 25th.—Letters of the 30th of December, received from Moodajee Boofla, con-
firming in the moft explicit terms the declaration
he had made fome weeks before in his letters to
Colonel Goddard and to the Governor; ftill
urging the neceffity of an accommodation with
the Poona government, and refufing to join the
Company's forces againft them. On this day
the Governor, notwithftanding his profeffed refolution not to anfwer Mr. Francis's Minute of
the 11th inftant, quotes and reprobates the opinion contained in it, in terms full of paffion and
contempt. Yet, with fo many new and mate-

rial

rial facts before him, with the certain knowledge of Moodajee Boofla's final refolutions, and of the meafures taken at Bombay, he himfelf propofes nothing, but leaves Colonel Goddard without orders or inftructions of any kind.

28th January.—Letters of the 12th of December, received from Bombay, advifing the Board that their forces, (amounting to 3410, officers included) had actually taken the field, to conduct Ragoba to Poona; that they had come to this refolution on the 12th of October; that they had concluded a new treaty with Ragoba; that their lateft intelligence from Europe gave them not the fmalleft apprehenfion of danger to Bombay in the abfence of their forces; that the whole conduct of their expedition was intrufted to a committee, confifting of Meffrs. Carnac, Egerton, and Moftyn; that whatever turn affairs might take at Poona, they fhould certainly require a confiderable augmentation of their force to defend the new acquifitions, and to garrifon Bombay; that Mr. Draper diffented from the whole of the meafure; and that Hyder Ally continued to fhew a difpofition very favourable to the French. They conclude with requefting Government to commence immediately fending them their annual fupply. In confequence of the preceding advices, the Governor promifed to lay fome propofitions before the Board in a few days,

* Vide Confultations 1ft Feb.   1ft

1ft February.—Letters of the 6th of January received from Colonel Goddard. He was ftill in the fame pofition at Huffunabad, on the banks of the Nerbudda, but propofed moving in a few days towards Poona. From an accurate map of the route, drawn by Mr. Smith, who accompanied Colonel Upton, the diftance between thefe two places appears to be about 470 Englifh miles.

By Colonel Goddard's laft letters it appears, that after croffing the river, he had deputed Lieutenant Weatherftone to Nagpour, in order to prefs Moodajee Boofla to conclude the treaty, and immediately to enter upon the execution of it, but without the fmalleft fuccefs: that he declined entering into a treaty, or taking any active part whatever till further accounts might arrive from Calcutta. To colour this refufal, Moodajee Boofla pleads the part taken by the Council of Bombay in favour of Ragoba: and folicits, as well as recommends, the relinquifh-ing the caufe of the latter, and accepting terms from the prefent minifterial party. It fhould be obferved, however, that Moodajee Boofla had taken his refolution long before it was poffible for him to have heard of the motions at Bombay. His letter to Colonel Goddard of the 23d of November is written in nearly the fame terms with thofe of the 30th of December, to Mr. Haftings; but the army did not move from Bombay before the 22d of November. It muft,

never-

nevertheless, be admitted, that the support given to Ragoba would naturally confirm Moodajee Boosla in his first resolution, considering that, as Colonel Goddard observes, " an attention to, " and observation of, the interest of both " would be an impracticable task to this Go- " vernment, and irreconcileable to themselves ; " and that Moodajee Boosla's views are incom- " patible with the measures now adopted in fa- " vour of Ragoba." The Court of Directors cannot fail of taking notice how often and how expresly this event was foretold by Mr. Francis. Goddard says, " that the schemes of the gentle- " men at Bombay, and the active part they " have taken in support of Ragoba, have de- " stroyed all hopes of concluding the proposed " alliance with the Court of Nagpour, until it " may be judged expedient by this government " to direct the former to be relinquished, in or- " der to leave room for the entire and free adop- " tion of the latter."

Whether this be a mere pretence or not, to excuse his refusal to accede to the proposed alliance, or whether he ever really formed the project attributed to him of asserting a claim to the supreme power of the Marhatta state, is much to be questioned. Colonel Goddard himself takes notice of *the inconsistency of his labouring so stre-nuously for the interest of the Peshwa, with whom he means soon to be engaged in hostilities,* and con-siders fiders his anfwer to this objection as *a refinement upon policy, that might almoft lead one to fufpect he was not altogether ferious, and determined upon his Sittarah expedition.*

By Mr. Weatherftone's letters to Colonel Goddard it appears, that the Government of Berar " were determined not to take any active " part whatever with the Company's armies; " that they had a thoufand arguments to oppofe " to thofe he urged in favour of the plan for " affuming the dignity of Rajah of Sittarah, " particularly the faith pledged, and the alli- " ance of friendfhip they had fworn with the " prefent Pefhwa; that their afferting their pre- " tenfions to the fovereignty would meet with " numberlefs oppofitions, and that a victory " could not be without fhedding much blood, " and at the expence of their violating the " facred engagements before entered into by " them." When the force and effect of thefe declarations are confidered, it will reft with Mr. Haftings to fatisfy the Company that his plan, ftated in the inftructions to Mr. Elliott, and in which he has embarked fo deeply, was not built without a foundation.

Mr. Weatherftone fays, that " the firft wifh " of that court feems now to fet afide our con- " nection with Ragoba; the fupporting of whom, " the Dewan faid, he was convinced was highly " impolitical,

" impolitical, and would in the end be fully
" proved fo; that that Chief was held in univer-
" fal abhorrence, and that the prejudices in the
" Decan againft him would not eafily, if ever,
" be removed."

The remainder of Mr. Weatherftone's letters
will be found to contain many particulars that
deferve the attention of the Court of.Directors;
efpecially a clear explanation of the views, principles, and policy of the Court of Nagpour,
of all which the Governor General does not appear to have had any precife information, or
any accurate idea. He concludes with faying,
" that the Rajah and Dewan expreffed a ftrong
" defire that the detachment might not move
" forward towards Poona, but remain in the
" neighbourhood of Berar," and in the mean
time be employed in conquering fome adjacent
diftricts for the Rajah's benefit. All the preceding letters were read in Council on the 1ft of
February, 1779, when the Governor faid, that
he had not had time to prepare the propofitions which he intended to lay before the Board.
His intentions, whatever they may be, have
not yet tranfpired; but no orders from hence
can now affect the motions of the detachment.
Suppofing Colonel Goddard to have marched on
the 12th of January, he ought to be at Poona
before any letters written at this time can reach
him. This Government have no other knowledge

ledge of the difficulties and oppofition he is likely to meet with, than what may be collected from Moodajee Boofla's letters. The Board is equally uninformed of the actual ftrength and condition of his army. On thefe points the Governor General obferves a profound filence. It may be concluded, however, from the refolution to fend two battalions, with a draft of 700 recruits to reinforce Colonel Goddard, that his army muft have fuffered confiderably by ficknefs or defertion. It is known that Captain Wray's regiment of cavalry was totally ruined, and that he and feveral other officers had obtained leave, under one pretence or other, to return to Bengal. Col. Goddard's public orders of the 1ft of November, accidentally produced at the Board of Ordnance by Colonel Pearfe, begin with declaring, that " the unmilitary and unex-
" ampled fpirit of difaffection to the fervice,
" which had fo manifeftly difplayed itfelf in
" the frequent defertions from the corps of ca-
" valry and infantry, within a few days, was
" become a matter of the moft ferious and im-
" portant confideration." There can be no doubt but his numbers muft be greatly reduced; nor is there any chance of his being joined by the reinforcement under Major Camac. When the detachment was ordered, it was fuppofed that a junction might be effected fomewhere in Berar. Colonel Goddard is now on his way to Poona; but whether Major Camac is to fol-

G   low

low him or not, is a point yet unknown to the Board.

On the 19th of December, the fuccefs of the enterprize againft Poona was ftill undetermined.

February 4th, 1779.—The Governor General lays his propofitions before the Board, for new inftructions to Colonel Goddard, and for refolutions on the late advices from Bombay. The form in which thefe voluminous papers are drawn up feems more than commonly loofe, confufed, and intricate. Whether they were intended to be fo, or whether they were haftily thrown together, without any fort of confideration or advice, may be doubted. Mr. Haftings's firft general object is to heap as much cenfure as poffible on the Prefidency of Bombay, as well for what they have themfelves done, as for the obftacles which, he fays, they have thrown in the way of his negociations with Moodajee Boofla; his fecond purpofe plainly appears to be, to break the treaty they have concluded with Ragoba, though certainly warranted, as he himfelf confeffes, by our letter to them of the 17th of Auguft, 1778; and to revert, if poffible, to his favourite alliance with the Rajah of Berar. To accomplifh this defign, he propofes that Colonel Goddard (whofe march to Poona he approves, though ftrictly not juftifiable under the laft orders of the Board of the

23d

23d of November) fhall continue to hold his command, independent of the Government of Bombay; that he may demand reinforcements from that Prefidency, which he was fent originally to reinforce, but thefe not to be commanded by any officer of a rank fuperior to his own; that he fhall be appointed the Minifter of this government at the court of Poona, independent of the Prefidency of Bombay; that he fhall demand of Ragoba a reimburfement of the expences of the expedition, at two lacks a month from the 1ft of June 1778, in addition to the fum of two lacks and a half, ftipulated by the treaty *in full*, for the expences of the Bombay army; that, in cafe of a refufal, he fhall either return to Berar, or retire to the lands ceded to the Company, which it feems are to be kept, notwithftanding the treaty is to be annulled; that the Prefidency of Bombay fhall be peremptorily required and commanded, in fuch cafe, to recall their troops from Poona, and from the Marhatta dominions; that the inftructions already given to Colonel Goddard do remain in full force, and that he be directed to refume the negociations with the Government of Berar, and to treat with it on the grounds of thefe inftructions, whenever an occafion fhall offer to execute them confiftently with the foregoing refolutions.

8th

· 8th February, 1779.—Mr. Wheler and Mr. Francis deliver their opinion at large, on the Governor's Propofitions; the Court of Directors will judge whether any thing advanced in fupport of them, either as fact or argument, remains unrefuted; the minutes will not admit of being abftracted, but it may be fufficient to ftate the general principles on which the propofitions are oppofed.

I. It is taken as a point admitted *in the Governor's own terms,* that the treaty with Ragoba is warranted by our inftructions; that it has received the firmeft and fulleft ratification that could be given to it by the contracting parties; and that it therefore can not admit either of amendment or addition.

II. It is contended that the additional demand, to be made by Colonel Goddard, is unjuft, and can never be admitted by Ragoba; and that, even were it granted, it would not amount to a reimburfement of our actual expence.

III. That the conditional order prefcribed to Colonel Goddard, and to the Prefidency of Bombay, in cafe of a refufal, are equivalent to a formal renunciation of the treaty.

IV. That the independent command, pretended to be vefted in Colonel Goddard, while

he

he co-operates with the Prefidency of Bombay, and acts on the fame grounds with theirarmy, is highly dangerous in itfelf, and canno take effect without fubverting the fundamenta principles of military difcipline and fubordincion.

V. That a junction of the two detachients, which thefe inftructions pofitively prelude, may, in fome cafes, be effential to their mutual fafety; and in many cafes neceffary to th fuccefs of their operations.

VI. That the vefting Colonel Goddar with feparate powers, from this government tc treat with the Court of Poona, independent of the Prefidency of Bombay, tends to reduc the credit and influence of that Prefidency, br no adequate or avowed object; and that it lands in direct contradiction to the Company's exprefs orders, given on occafion of the feparate powers delegated to Colonel Upton *.

VII. That an attempt to renew the negociation with Moodajee Boofla, befides all former objections to the meafure, is not warranted by the experience the Board have had of his character and difpofition, or by the treatment already received from him; nor can it be reconciled to the late treaty with Ragoba.

* Vide General Letter 7th February, 1777, Paragr. 21, 22, 23, 24.

In

In te face of thefe, and many other arguments the propofitions were voted by Mr. Barwell ad Mr. Haftings, without reply.

9th February.—The Governor's letter of this
date to Moodajee Boofla contains fome remarkable pffages. He laments, rather than com-
plains of the *diftruft* entertained by that Chief;
and "declares that, had he accepted of the terms
" offeed him by Colonel Goddard, and con-
" clued a treaty with this government. upon
" then, he fhould have held the obligation of
" it fiperior to that of any engagement formed
" by the Government of Bombay; and fhould
" have thought it his duty to maintain it, &c.
" againft every confideration, *even of the moft*
" *vaiuable interefts and fafety of the Englifh pof-*
" *feffans intrufted to his charge.*" At the fame
time, however, he reminds him, " That the
" original intention of fending an Englifh army
" fron this to the Weftern fide of India, was
" to affift the Government of Bombay in the
" accomplifhment of a plan concerted with
" the actual rulers of the Marhatta State."—
He concludes with profeffing, that his difpofition and wifhes remain the fame; that nothing
is yet loft; and that he wifhes to be guided by
Moodajee Boofla's inclinations.

In the Governor's minute, recorded the 15th
of February, and Mr. Francis's, recorded the

2d

2d of March, the general fubject of the negociations with Ragoba and Moodajee Boofla, and the march of the two armies, is thoroughly difcuffed; and fuch lights thrown upon the whole tranfaction, as leave no doubt concerning the true motives of the perfons engaged in it.

25th February, 1779.— The Governor lays before the Board a paper received the day before from Madras, containing intelligence of the defeat of the Bombay army near Poona; which he fays, he believes to be *but too true*; but does not think proper to propofe any immediate meafures to be taken in confequence.

Mr. Francis, finding no propofition made by the Governor, moves that orders be fent to General Stibbert, to put him on his guard, and to hold the troops ftationed in Rohilcund, and in Owde, in readinefs to march.—The motion was oppofed both by Mr. Barwell and the Governor, as *unneceffary and unreafonable*; and the Governor faid, he wifhed it had not been made; yet in the end, it was agreed to, with an amendment propofed by Barwell, which carried the principle of the motion much farther than Mr. Francis intended, viz. " That the two brigades " fhould be immediately affembled and en- " camped."

Mr.

Mr. Francis ftated the evident contradiction contained in the arguments ufed by the Majority, and oppofed the amendment.

1ft March, 1779.—Letters of the 7th of February from Fort St. George, and of the 26th of January from Colonel Goddard, were read at the Board; the former was figned by Sir Eyre Coote, and ftates in ftrong terms the fatal confequences likely to attend the difafter at Poona, particularly to that government. They obferve, that " by one ill-timed and un-" fortunate enterprize the reputation of our " arms is fullied, and the friendfhip of the " principal Indian ftates hazarded, or loft for " ever ; and that too at a period when we are " engaged in a war which calls for the exer-" tion of all our force, and the good-will of " every ftate in alliance with us." In the conclufion, they recommended to the Board to direct Colonel Goddard's retreat through Berar, towards the coaft of Orixa, and the Northern Circars.

By Colonel Goddard's letter it appears, that he was uninformed of the event at Poona; he inclofes a letter of the 11th of January from General Carnac and Colonel Egerton, in which they advife him to proceed either to Broach or Surat, or to remain on the borders of Berar; but do not defire him to advance towards Poona.

Poona.—He himfelf is of opinion, " That a
" profpect of being able to effect the revolution
" in favour of Ragoba themfelves, is their mo-
" tive for expreffing fo little anxiety about the
" arrival of the detachment."

The Governor, without propofing any in-
ftruction for Colonel Goddard, moved that General Stibbert fhould be ordered to fend the firft
brigade acrofs the Jumna, and to encamp it on
the other fide. Mr. Francis expreffed, at once,
his fenfe of the meafure ; but defired that the
further confideration of it might be put off till
the next morning : This was agreed to by the
Governor, on condition that he might be allowed an opportunity of confidering Mr. Francis's objections to the motion, before they were
brought into debate at the Board. Mr. Wheler
and Mr. Francis, concurring in opinion, drew
up their reafons in the form of a joint proteft,
which they fent next morning to the Governor,
about an hour before the Council met.

2d March, 1779.—The Governor began by
declaring, that he had not read the joint proteft ; and delivered in a minute, retracting that
of yefterday. The minutes on both fides deferve attention, but cannot eafily be abftracted.

When the bufinefs was over, Mr. Francis,
finding that no inftructions were intended for
Colonel Goddard, moved that orders fhould be
H   fent

fent him immediately to retire to Berar, and from thence towards the coaft of Orixa, and the Chicacole Sarcar, fuppofing always that he fhould not have reached the other fide of India before he received thefe orders: The motion, it was agreed, fhould lie for confideration.

4th March, 1779.—The debate of this day, in confequence of which Mr. Francis's propofition was rejected by the majority, will be found to throw confiderable light upon the political views and principles of Mr. Haftings. He objects to the motion for two reafons: 1ft, Becaufe he thinks it probable that Colonel Goddard has refumed his negociation with Moodajee Boofla: 2dly, Becaufe the propofed route lay through the dominions of the Nizam; " who, it is not to be expected would " confent to their paffage ; nor is this a time " to furnifh him with a pretext for open ho- " ftilities againft the Government." Yet the negociations which Colonel Goddard is fuppofed to have refumed, and which Mr. Haftings thinks it unfafe to interrupt, have the invafion of the Nizam's dominions for one of . its principal objects,

In the remainder of the Governor's minute, the Court of Directors will fee, that conqueft and extenfion of dominion are now his profeffed and avowed objects ; and that Mr. Francis, in endeavouring to confine the Company's armies

armies within their actual possessions, is supposed to prescribe *narrow limits* to this Government. The minute recorded by Mr. Francis on the 8th of March contains every thing that appeared to him necessary for the general defence of his motion, or to refute the general doctrines advanced and maintained by Mr. Hastings.

Mr. Francis concluding, from some words which fell from the Governor in reply to the first motion, that his principal objection lay against moving the detachment towards the Chicacole Sarcar, and wishing at all events to withdraw the detachment from a situation of danger into the country of a friend, moved again that Colonel Goddard might be ordered to retreat into Berar. This proposition, however, met with the same fate with the preceding; but whether the arguments, used against the second motion can be reconciled to those which were employed against the first, deserves consideration. In this place, however, it is material to be observed, that, supposing any future turn of events should, in the eyes of those who judge only by events, render it a fortunate circumstance that Colonel Goddard should have proceeded to Surat, Mr. Hastings will have no merit to claim from that measure, or from any advantageous consequences which

may

may attend it. In this *day's debate, he exprefsly fays, "That he wifhes equally with Mr.
" Francis, for the return of the detachment to
" Berar, and equally dreads to hear of its pro-
" ceeding to the other coaft."

In the fame debate he obferved that the plan
for reftoring Ragoba to the adminiftration of the
Government at Poona had failed, and that Colonel Goddard therefore, from the inftant he received certain advice of that conclufion, was
under *exprefs orders* to recur to his negociations
with Moodajee Boofla, which neceffarily and
unavoidably implied his return to Berar. It
will hereafter appear that Colonel Goddard received thanks and rewards for taking that very
ftep, which, according to Mr. Haftings's prefent declaration, muft be contrary to the exprefs
orders of the Board. Admitting that Colonel
Goddard was juftified by the neceffity of his
fituation, in proceeding by forced marches to
Surat, as foon as he had heard of the defeat
near Poona, Mr. Haftings clearly has no fhare
in the merit of that refolution, or in any good
confequences that might have attended it, fince,
according to his exprefs orders, Colonel Goddard ought to have returned to Berar.

March 10th, 1779. ‡ —Letter received from
Col. Goddard, dated the 5th of February, from

* 4th March, 1779.
‡ Extract upon Confultations 11th March.

Brampour;

Brampour; in which he fays, he was determined to move next day towards Surat, according to orders he had received from the Select Committee at Bombay; who, on the 22d of January, tell him, they are not able to give him any precife information as to the reafons of the return of their army, or the probable confequences of it.

Colonel Goddard arrived at Surat about the 26th of February; having not feen an enemy, nor met with any oppofition whatever, in his march from Brampour. In his laft letter, dated at Surat, on the 28th of October, 1779, he informs the Board, that the Minifter of the Peifhaw had, in plain and direct terms, declared to him, in the name of his Mafter, that he would not accede to the propofals he (Colonel Goddard) had made him, or conclude peace with the Englifh, unlefs Ragoba was delivered up to him, and Salfette reftored to the Marhatta Government.

In confequence of this declaration, Colonel Goddard had broken off the negociation, and propofed fetting out for Bombay immediately, to concert the plan of future operations with the Select Committee there.

That Committee, in their letter of the 31ft of October, 1779, inform the Governor Gene-
neral,

neral, and Council, that they had ſtrongly recommended to General Goddard not to preci-
pitate matters, but to endeavour to gain time,
and defer any declaration until they were in
a better condition for an active war.

F I N I S.

www.ingramcontent.com/pod-product-compliance
Lightning Source LLC
Chambersburg PA
CBHW031249260626
47169CB00007B/2505